Improving Intercultural Learning Experiences in Higher Education
Responding to cultural scripts for learning

Thushari Welikala and Chris Watkins

Institute of Education
University of London

First published in 2008 by the Institute of Education, University of London,
20 Bedford Way, London WC1H 0AL
www.ioe.ac.uk/publications

British Library Cataloguing in Publication Data
A catalogue record for this publication is available from the British Library

ISBN 978 0 85473 804 5

Page make up by Keystroke, 28 High Street, Tettenhall, Wolverhampton
Printed by Elanders, Merlin Way, New York Business Park, North Tyneside NE27 0QG

'It is excellent to see this new guide to intercultural learning issues. A timely contribution to the expanding debate on academic transition and intercultural learning.'

Dominic Scott, Chief Executive, UK Council for
International Student Affairs (UKCISA)

'This book draws attention in a very general and widely applicable way to the experiences of overseas students in the UK and suggests ways in which cultural and other misunderstandings that often arise can be overcome. It is thus essential reading for teachers and also students and others involved in higher education in the UK today, which as well as widening participation to new groups of home students, now also includes many more overseas students. Thushari Welikala and Chris Watkins draw attention to commonalities in the experiences of these new students in the new higher education.'

Patrick Ainley, Professor of Training and Education,
University of Greenwich and Convenor of the Society for Research
into Higher Education's Student Experience Network

'In the global village that higher education has become, international students often find challenges as they encounter new pedagogic styles in which they are expected to give an account of themselves. However, these students also bring with them often untapped resources which could, if encouraged forward, widen the educational experiences of all students. That is one of the messages of this important booklet. In articulating, and demonstrating the educational potential of, the concept of "cultural scripts", Welikali and Watkins have actually performed here a service for higher education worldwide.'

Ronald Barnett, Pro-Director (Longer Term Strategy) and Professor
of Higher Education, Institute of Education, University of London

'The exploration of cultural scripts for learning enables a rich and nuanced understanding of how international students experience higher education. The students' voices in this book provide a powerful insight into their learning experiences. The careful interpretations of these experiences as presented by the authors will be invaluable for anyone working with international students.'

Dr Kelly Coate, Lecturer in Teaching and Learning in
Higher Education, Centre for Excellence in Learning and
Teaching (CELT), National University of Ireland, Galway

Contents

Figures

Introduction

For many decades people from all parts of the world have come to the UK to study. In recent years numbers have increased and arguably greater attention has been given to their experience of being a student. The British Council has offered valuable guidance on issues of cultural awareness (2007). However, the focus of such guidance can be every aspect of a student's experience **except** aspects of their learning encounters.

This book represents an attempt to share the understandings from an empirical study conducted with international postgraduate students learning in a particular institution of higher education in the UK (Welikala, 2006). The study gathered very rich data from 40 respondents through a process of active interviewing (Holstein and Gubrium, 1995). The analysis of this data was carried out through constructivist grounded theory (Charmaz, 2000).

The book considers these key questions.

- In what ways do cultures of learning vary?

- What do international students tell us about the experience of learning in the UK, and what happens if their current experience differs from their previous experiences of learning?

- Can experiences of learning be improved? How and by whom?

- What might intercultural learning be and how might it help?

Core concepts

Everyone grows up in a culture, and in so doing we – wittingly or other-wise – may adopt the views of learning which are prevalent. But this is not a fixed process; we may have experiences which help us beyond our culture, so we must not view culture as deterministic for the individual. Indeed we all know of examples of cultures changing, so we must view culture as a dynamic, rather than a static, notion. The stance adopted in the study on which we base our discussion here is to view culture as 'the ensemble of stories we tell ourselves about ourselves' (Geertz, 1975: 448), so the learning culture comprises the stories told about learning. These stories have significant effect, especially on the way learners go about their learning. Hence the empirical study on which this book is based also uses the notion of 'cultural script'.

The concept of cultural script

The core concept of script has proved important in our understanding of human behaviour. It offers a way of understanding human patterns without limiting them to rules and schemas of a rigid sort. Since Schank and Abelson (1977) the idea of script has helped to comprehend human memory, the organisation of knowledge and human action. We know that memory operates in the form of meaningful 'stories', not merely decontextualised information.

A script is an ordered sequence of actions appropriate to a particular context and related to some purpose. It spells out the roles and mean-ingful behaviours which would be expected according to that script, and informs action when such events are met again (Nelson, 1986).

We develop and apply our scripts in a range of life contexts: family (Atwood, 1996), organisations (Lord and Kernan, 1987), and the wider culture. 'Cultural scripts' is the term used by linguists to denote ways of speaking (Wierzbicka, 1998), but more widely the term denotes the meanings and actions we learn from cultural experience (Azuma, 2001).

In the educational context, international research on teaching has explained commonalities in and across countries as a teaching script (Stigler and Hiebert, 1998). Very few studies have focused on learners' scripts, the exception being those which investigate newcomers learning the script of the classroom (Fivush, 1984, Cullen and St. George, 1996). Some very recent work addresses the context of multicultural classrooms from this perspective (de Haan and Elbers, 2008).

In the study on which this book is based, cultural scripts reflect generalised action knowledge, which informs how someone makes meaning of a situation and which also guides their action in a particular context.

Such scripts can be shown to be culturally shared, especially when someone offers a comment of the sort: 'We [cultural group] don't go about it that way'.

Such comments highlight that people sometimes use categorisations of themselves as members of a cultural group. 'In our country, we . . .'; 'We Japanese are . . .'; and so on. But it appears that when people use such language they are not being deterministic or overly categorical, because they also know of exceptions to the broad patterns they are reporting. Similarly, when this book reports the voices of particular learners, it does so by referring to their name and their country, thus mentioning the individual and their context. This practice should not be taken to mean that the authors – or the respondents – think that national cultures exist in some uniform or fixed way, or that we are categorising respondents in some rigid fashion. All we have done is to offer examples of cultural scripts which emerge in reflective interview conversations with people from many countries.

Focusing on cultural scripts for learning does not ignore the fact that variations in learning scripts can be present within cultures. Hence, the authors do not attempt to emphasise diversities in learning scripts only as cross-cultural phenomena. The meaning of culture adopted here also reflects that we do not compartmentalise cultures within geographical locations and we write with the awareness that different scripts for learning exist in various cultural strata within cultures as well as across cultures.

3

Finally, we are happy to accept that some of the scripts identified among students coming to the UK are also evident with 'home' or 'native' students, among whom there would also be variation. But as the study gathered evidence only from learners coming to the UK, we will not comment on this.

Our main focus in this book, then, is to discuss the varying cultural scripts that learners bring into learning situations, with specific interest in the impact of such variations on the act of learning.

1 Learning we bring from home

It is not simply overseas students encounter different ways of teaching and different expectations about learning; rather such encounters are juxtaposed with the cultures of learning they bring with them.

Cortazzi and Jin, 1997: 83–4

Learners from various cultures do not leave their cultural scripts for learning at home, merely because they are embarking on a sojourn of learning in a different culture.

But what do we know about the views of learning they bring from a range of cultures? Learning is essentially cultural and social, as well as personal. It is informed by views about what constitutes acceptable knowledge, how this knowledge comes to be known and how knowledge is to be communicated. Do these things vary in different cultures?

This chapter highlights the ways in which learners from a range of cultures may have their own cultural ways of approaching learning. In the empirical study, varying cultural scripts were identified in the areas illustrated in figure 1.1 on p. 6.

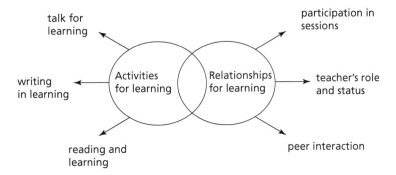

Figure 1.1 Cultural scripts for learning: main areas

These variations seemed to reflect differences in:

- the perception of the role of the learner
- the views about knowledge and how knowledge is constructed.

Talk for learning

All teaching–learning situations depend on communication. But different learners may have grown up with different scripts regarding the importance of talking for learning. Who should talk, when one should talk and what should be spoken seem to have intertwined with varying cultural scripts which are related to talking. These scripts can influence any teaching–learning situation, and imply different views on the meaning of such situations, as well as the role of the learner and the teacher.

It's the teacher's job to talk

Students from some cultures see the classroom as a place where active vocal participation by students is not proper. According to such cultures, the teacher holds the sole authority of knowledge, and so teaching–learning situations are supposed to provide the learners with the knowledge expertise of the teacher. It becomes the teacher's job to talk and the learner's job to listen:

> We never interrupt the teacher, because if you interrupt in the
> middle of the lesson, you cannot learn properly (Anita, Italy).

The way the teachers are perceived is associated with a view of knowledge:

> Back home, things are always black and white. This is the absolute
> right and this is the absolute wrong. So, we do not argue or question
> the teacher's knowledge. What is the point? Teacher gives the
> answer at the end . . . we are not very much bothered to look for
> alternatives to what the teacher says (Jordan, Nigeria).

According to Jordan, the process of learning means knowing the 'right' answers to questions. One of the main responsibilities of the teacher within such a context of learning is to know the right answers, which are out there, and then to 'deliver' them to the learners. This context does not seem to encourage the learners to critically explore alternative views about the process of making knowledge. Hence, critical participation through discussion and arguments is not seen as necessary to or enriching the pedagogic situations.

In addition, some cultural scripts about who should talk link to cultural perceptions of other important people – adults and parents:

> We wait for the information to come from the teacher. Here it is the
> job of the learner. There, we think, 'I am here, so teach me. I am
> listening' . . . in my culture, we are trained to listen to adults and
> parents. No questions. This transfers into the school and then to the
> university (Lee, Hong Kong).

Thus, the role of the learner as a listener is informed by the role of the teacher as an adult in society. This suggests how cultural scripts may span different contexts within the same culture – from a larger society to the context of home, school and university. At the same time, we do not generalise too quickly or stereotype a country; there is evidence that many first-year university students in Hong Kong understand autonomous learning, and find it an attractive proposition, even though they have had little previous experience of it (Chan, 2001).

Critical talking is not very ethical

Some cultural scripts for learning lead participants to perceive critical engagement according to a set of cultural and social ethics of being a learner as well as a social being.

> We never argue when the teacher says something. Nobody would like it, since we are not supposed to disagree and argue with the teacher. We have to respect them. They are our Gurus (Rani, Mauritius).

Some learners avoid engaging in a process of argumentation, especially with the teacher and even with peers in front of the teacher. This may be the case at university level. For them, the process of coming to know is strongly embedded in their relationship with the teacher. The teacher–student relationship in certain cultures seems to have been shaped largely by the ascribed status of the role of the teacher as well as the feelings embedded in the role relationship.

Being critical as confronting others' viewpoints

The act of being critical within teaching–learning situations is also viewed as an act that is informed by norms and ethics related to maintaining good social relations within a society:

> We are not for this arguing, questioning and critically reviewing others' point of view in the class. That is our culture. . . . The majority of the students do not think that talking inside the class and arguing with each other is necessary (Sheng-yu, China).

The act in some cultures of critically reviewing one's point of view does not seem to be detached from certain sensitivities attached to human relationships in the wider society. Hence, critical interaction for learning is given meaning in terms of the act of confronting others, which does not contribute to healthy human relationships. In this way, critical participation for learning is not necessarily considered a positive practice by learners who come with different cultural scripts for talking to learn in UK universities.

> Be critical, be critical . . . we do not talk and that is how we are. The Japanese, the Chinese, yes, we are self-critical. We do not go on criticising others . . . do not criticise others openly. We do not like confrontation with the others (Akihiro, Japan).

Here we can see that, for some learners, to be vocally and critically interactive for the purpose of learning is not merely viewed as an act in learning, but can relate to other important cultural scripts, with which they live in a range of cultural contexts.

Writing in learning

Writing as reproducing

Writing does not hold the same connotations across cultures. Learners from different cultures appear to have varying ways of making sense of writing for academic purposes.

In some cultures of learning, writing refers to writing answers, reproducing the notes of the teacher or reproducing facts learnt from other texts:

> We always reproduce what the teacher has dictated to us. . . . For essay writing we had some almost fixed set of topics such as national heroes, healthy mind in a healthy body . . . we memorise an essay written on these topics from a text. Then reproduce it as an essay . . . when we write we are descriptive. We have to be careful about what we write and how we write. . . . We cannot critically evaluate others' view. That is dangerous in our culture (Abaz, Pakistan).

For some learners, their main focus in writing is to (re)produce a descriptive piece of writing rather than being critical, analytical or evaluative. This particularly cultural way of writing for academic purposes is shaped by the examination-oriented education systems, where the learner is supposed to write answers. Apart from the examination orientation, the practice of doing descriptive academic writing is intertwined with the meanings and norms of going about social interactions in the larger society. As in talk, critical analysis of others' point of view in writing is informed by cultural scripts about the wider social relationships among members in some cultures.

According to some learners, their ways of going about writing for academic purposes are directly informed by their particular system of education:

> We always rote learn the teacher's notes. We do not think critically what the teacher is talking about. Even when we read them later, we do not think of the notes critically. . . . We just write them down at examinations without thinking too much (Freeda, Cyprus).

Learners who come from examination-oriented learning cultures frame their scripts for writing in such a way so that they can achieve success within that particular culture of learning. Their understanding that reproducing the teacher's notes is sufficient to get through the examination discourages critical engagement with the act of writing.

We write like we speak

Learners' cultural scripts for writing can be intertwined with their cultural scripts for speaking, which then influence their use of writing for learning. In some cultures, saying things directly or talking to the point is considered impolite. Hence, the cultural script for talking encourages people to talk around the particular topic before they come to the main focus of a particular conversation:

> In our culture, writing is spiral. Here, the first sentence is the main point. But in Japan, the main point comes towards the end. First, we just go around the main focus and then only we write to the point. Do not need to support all what we say. We are good at describing things.
> Even while talking, these English people are arguing critically. They talk as if they are writing an assignment. We never do that (Akihiro, Japan).

How some learners structure an academic piece of writing seems to have been shaped by their cultural scripts for speaking. Thus, some learners feel uncomfortable in starting an academic writing task with the main focus. Similarly to their practice in speaking, they like to build up the related context of the particular writing task first, and then move on to the main focus. Such cultural scripts for writing for academic purposes imply that to address the main focus of a writing task at the beginning and then build up an argument is by no means a cultural universal:

> N . . . aaaa . . . ow, when we want to say certain things . . . in my culture, we go round and round and raaa..ound before coming to the exact point. . . . You know, we never say things directly and we apply the same thing in writing as well.
> These [English] people are very direct . . . never beat around the bush when they talk. But we always do. We form our written language also in that manner (Seema, Brazil).

Writing language to feel

Learners' choice of words and styles of expression also seem to reflect their culture:

> Back home, we use lots of adjectives and vivid language. We use the language to feel. Academic or not, any writing should be written in a reader-friendly manner. But here you cannot use even 'I'. It is very objective. We never write like this (Gifti, Jamaica).

It appears that the meaning of writing and the norms and beliefs regarding how to write do not show a unifying relationship across cultures. Some cultures prefer vivid, sensuous language to objective ways of writing and they employ this kind of language in academic writing. This further suggests that the idea of 'reader-friendliness' in writing reflects different meanings in different cultures of learning.

> You know, what we mean by academic writing can be somewhat different. The thing is that we have more space in writing – we can use words much more freely to convey the kind of message we want to convey. Here, all the time it is about being objective . . . a kind of rigid structure (Saman, Sri Lanka).

What is accepted as academic writing in one particular culture may be interpreted as a rigid way of doing writing by a learner who is exposed to a much more flexible way of expressing ideas within academia.

Critiquing as personal attack

For other learners, referring to others' texts in writing is seen as high-lighting only the positive aspects of those texts. According to their cultural ethics and beliefs 'constructive criticism' is regarded as a personal attack on the author.

> In my culture, we always look for the positive things. We compare
> others' work to see why this is better than that. . . . We do not
> criticise negatively . . . they think . . . if you criticise . . . you are doing
> personal attack. So, we just mention their names (Yasin, Taiwan).

Learners who come from such cultures believe that they review the
author rather than the author's point of view:

> What I think about their [the authors'] writing is not important. They
> [the teachers in the home culture] do not care about what I think of
> the writer. Here, all the time, you have to say 'in my point of view'
> (Magi, France).

This implies that some cultures of learning do not encourage learners
to critically engage with the author's point of view. Hence, they believe
that texts should be read in terms of the meanings constructed by the
author.

Some learners indicate that although relating critically to others'
viewpoints while writing is not a script in their cultures of learning,
they start to see something of value in it:

> You see, I am used to write in a different manner. Back home, we
> may use quotations, just write the name of the author underneath
> . . . and that is it. We do not normally be critical of what another
> writer has said in relation to what I am writing. Here, you need to be
> conscious of what you are writing. It connects me to other people's
> thinking (Oliver, Malawi).

Regarding references

Interestingly, the concept of using references in academic writing is
perceived differently by learners from different cultures.

> When we write we are not much bothered about giving reference to
> all what we write. Sometimes, we give reference to . . . like when we
> directly quote . . . otherwise we just write, [we] do not write 'I got
> this idea from that one' and so on (Pamela, Finland).

13

> When we write back home . . . you can write others' ideas as if they
> are your own. You are not required to refer to all what you say in a
> piece of writing (Jordan, Nigeria).

Thus, the idea of using references in academic writing seems to be interpreted in many different ways in different cultures. In certain cultures, producing a successful piece of academic writing is not associated with relating the ideas in the argument to their sources. Their argument is that one should have the freedom to use the knowledge gained from other sources, adjust them accordingly, and produce them freely.

Reading for learning

Reading for academic purposes seems to be practised with varying meanings in different cultures.

Reading the author

For some learners the act of reading is one of receiving the meanings constructed by the author, and texts are taken to comprise one single meaning.

> In reading . . . we do differently. . . . They [our teachers] want us to
> read for information. I am used to read just what is there in the text.
> No arguments with the text (Magi, France).

In this view, reading is a neutral act, a receptive task of getting the information given in a text by a particular author.

> We read what is there in the text. What else? (Anita, Italy).

Critical engagement with the viewpoints of the author seems a novel experience for some learners. Rather than being engaged in critical dialogue with the writer's viewpoint, they seem to agree with the meanings conveyed by the author in a particular text.

Interpretations other than those from the author's viewpoint are regarded as additions to the 'correct' meaning of a text.

Reading the Gestalt

The idea of reading in parts or scanning texts for specific purposes is not seen as valuable in some cultures of learning.

> We need to get the whole story rather than getting chunks . . . if I give my opinion after reading a bit, I am not giving the truth . . . not making sense of what the author is really saying. I am fantasising . . . adding too much for my interpretation. . . . You see, I am not used to this bits and pieces reading (Roger, Ghana).

Emphasis on getting the 'whole' meaning of a text implies that there are varying meanings surrounding the purpose of reading for academic purposes as well as around the role of the author in constructing a particular text. For instance, here, the role of the author is assumed to provide the reader with the 'truth', the whole truth about a particular area of knowledge, while the main task of the reader is to understand this single truth by skimming the text from beginning to end. Within this context, critical dialogue with the author's point of view is not considered significant.

> Reading for us means to read the whole story. I do not know how we can just read a chapter or two and get what is there in the book. What is this scaaa…nning or something? (Yasin, Taiwan).

Some cultures believe that texts themselves carry meaning. Hence, the main purpose of reading is getting information rather than constructing meaning out of the written text.

The teacher's role

Alongside the activities for learning, and the meanings these activities hold, are the relations that any learner encounters. Foremost among these are the relations with teachers and the view of the role which such teachers play. Among different cultures there appear different scripts for making meaning of and acting towards teachers.

The respected guru

Some cultures hold that the teacher is not only the expert source from whom to gain knowledge, but also someone who holds a recognised position in the community as an adult who has ongoing influence through their moral and intellectual guidance.

> We still obey the morals and the values and I think respecting teachers is there in our blood. Think now, if we meet one of our teachers, who has got retired, what kind of feelings do we get? It is more a spiritual thing I believe . . . teacher–pupil relation is a very sensitive issue in our culture (Saman, Sri Lanka).

Within this context, the teacher is viewed in some ways as a parent. Respecting and obeying the teacher is considered as a way of paying gratitude to the kind of knowledge and moral guidance they provide for the life of the learners. Therefore, the role relations between the teacher and student, as well as the status of the role of the teacher, are multifaceted and complex. The role of the teacher in such cultures does not confine itself to a particular pedagogic situation.

Forms of address that are used may reflect the kind of relationship that learners in some cultures maintain with the teacher.

> We consider the teachers to be our adults who should be treated respectfully. It is a shame that the teachers are called just by their half names, Jack, Pat (Viola, Fiji).

Some learners are very conscious about other details in the teacher–student relationship, from the way of expressing one's own views in front of the teachers to the way one should dress for classrooms. Such considerations inform learners' behaviour.

> In our culture, the teachers are very supportive. But we respect them and do not like to argue with them and go against their point of view openly. So, the learners can discuss during the lessons but we have to think about what we are talking (Gifti, Jamaica).

Questioning and arguing with and in front of the teacher are related to the ethical issues embedded in the teacher–student relationship:

> Back home, we are free to ask questions from the teacher. But, never like this. . . . We never just go on talking in the middle of the lesson. . . . Even if we disagree with the teacher, we will not argue with the teacher in the classroom. It is not nice. If we want to talk . . . we may meet him later . . . we have the discipline thing in behaving with the teachers. If we argue like this, they will not like it . . . think that we are at them (John, Kenya).

Hence, learners' silence during pedagogic encounters should not be misunderstood as passive learning. In some cultures of learning, formal teaching–learning situations are not the right situations for questioning. The act of behaving as a learner is embedded in various other social ethics and norms. It is a rather different way of behaving as a learner, as well as respecting the knowledge and status of the teacher. For learners with such cultural scripts, learning is a significant cultural–social act, not merely a way of improving knowledge or gaining qualifications.

Teacher in the community

> We have the rapport all the time. We meet the teacher on the road, in the market place, we call them, 'hi sir, how are you?' . . . We have that bond with the teacher. It is not just teaching something and

17

vanishing. He is there, in the community living with you (Oliver, Malawi).

In some cultures the role responsibilities of the teacher transcend institutional responsibilities, to encompass being an active member of the community. In these cultures the boundaries of the role go beyond working according to a particular job description:

> Here, the teacher–pupil relation is just simple. You teach, and go. Teachers in China are better. They are the authorities in our culture . . . have the power to change things for the future. More responsible regarding the future of the students . . . we listen to the students . . . understand their problems, and be moral guides to them (Sheng-yu, China).

So the role of the teacher extends beyond the four walls of the classroom to the wider community. Apart from the responsibility of making people knowledgeable, the teacher has a moral responsibility for his or her student as a human being, a member of a wider society. Interestingly, the last respondent is also a teacher in her home country, so can report on the other side of the picture:

> I would not talk with them as if I am a friend. It is just spiritual. (I) like to maintain my space as a teacher.

The authority in this version of the teacher's role does not result in a morally or spiritually detached relationship between teacher and student. While teachers and learners are not equals in status, the relationship is not highlighted by power in authority, more by the desire to 'maintain the space' of teaching within an important broader context of connection.

Teacher as expert; respected for knowledge authority

In some other cultures knowledge expertise is the main reason to respect teachers.

> Most of the teachers in our society think that they are superior to us, have higher positions and . . . important . . . I think that they are experts and have to be respected and listened to (Freeda, Cyprus).

Within this type of cultural context, learners appear to be respecting the knowledge authority, and follow the social norm of respecting the teacher because of what knowledge has ascribed to them. The respect for teachers is almost a social obligation.

In some cultures the role of the teacher is respected with some detachment:

> In our culture, the teachers . . . are specialists of the subject they teach . . . have qualifications . . . they have the authority and they take decisions. I do not think that apart from the power or the expertise of knowledge they have, there is anything else to respect in them (Magi, France).

Here, the learners make sense of the respect they have for teachers in relation to the power and authority teachers hold within the classroom owing to their qualifications. The role relations between the teacher and the student seem to be somewhat detached; the obligations of the teacher do not seem to permeate into society but are limited to teaching–learning situations. These views shape the teacher–student role relationships as they are played out during teaching–learning situations.

Peer interactions

Peer interaction for learning has been given strong significance in some circles, some academic viewpoints and some institutions. But no matter how much focus is given by educationists to peer interaction for learning, when the context of learning comprises multiple cultures, peer interaction seems to hold varying degrees of importance.

Interaction as a bonus

Some students, in the process of learning, embrace interaction among their peers as a positive means of getting support and sharing knowledge. They further believe that supporting each other and working in peer groups is an individual responsibility of learners, especially when they are learning in multicultural contexts (Hvitfeldt, 1986).

> From human perspective, it is common to care and share the problems and help someone in need. . . . Being among friends is a big bonus. In our culture, if you ask for help, someone will stop his work and help you (Abaz, Pakistan).

Such cultures of learning seem to encourage learning with and from peers, forming informal peer groups for learning.

Interaction as hindrance

Other cultures believe in learners being more isolated. They may highlight competition; for example, competition among learners for qualifications, or even competition between cultural groups. Such scripts may encourage learners to act alone:

> We compete with each other for learning, for qualifications . . . very lonely as learners competing with each others . . . the Chinese in our culture . . . they really conquer the field of science and maths. So, we are trying our best to learn (Raju, Malaysia).

So learners in some cultures may willingly avoid interaction for learning. This may even be the case for learning in cultures that are very collective in other domains. For instance, learners from Cyprus, Sri Lanka, India and elsewhere reported that they prefer to learn individually, rather than collectively in groups. Two reasons were given. The first was that of competition among learners for qualifications. When many learners compete with each other for a few better places in society, they seem to remain aloof as learners. The second was the exam orientation that is dominant in a particular system of education. If examinations are deemed to distil the 'best' through the marks achieved, then sharing knowledge is viewed as helping others to get more marks. Therefore, treasuring one's own knowledge and skills to be reproduced in examinations is the safest way to score the best marks.

Interaction as losing face

There are other instances when students describe peer interaction for learning as a disadvantage. For example, some Chinese people feel that discussing problems in learning with peers is a means of 'losing face' or losing 'Mianzi'.

> We do not normally discuss about our problems or whatever with the
> friends. It is considered a kind of losing face. I know there are two
> girls in my class from our country and they have many problems with
> language. And they know very well that I am a lecturer in English.
> But they never ever talk about their difficulties with me. That is the
> way we are (Sheng-Yu, China).

Since losing face is losing the predictability in social roles and relations, it would also make sense that learners with such cultural scripts would make an effort to save face in front of their peers. This may well inform their roles during discussion-based teaching.

Thus, in terms of learning, different cultures make sense of interaction in different ways. Some cultural scripts for learning encourage learners to embrace interaction among peers as a positive means of learning, while other cultural scripts discourage peer interaction as a means of disturbance in achieving their personal targets of learning.

So far . . .

Chapter 1 illustrates the fact that different activities involved in learning do not reflect one single meaning across cultures. The acts of talking, writing and reading for learning in higher education are differently viewed from the standpoint of different cultural scripts. The views of role relations and role expectations regarding teachers as well as peers also vary remarkably among different cultures. These different cultural scripts for learning considerably influence and shape the learner's act of learning as well as his or her conception of learning.

It is important to emphasise that we have not been categorising learners in cultural compartments in any rigid way. When exploring cultural scripts for learning we have not found it possible to categorise learners and how they learn according to where they come from. Differences between learners do not easily fall into geographical or other categories based on nationality (e.g. Asian–European), or any other of the categories that are given to whole societies (for example, collectivist–individualistic societies).

But there remains something important about the fact that we – and the students themselves – have been identifying scripts as cultural scripts. By the fact that these ways of approaching learning are felt to be part of one's culture, they may have a different importance from other scripts; for example, those which could be identified as idiosyncratic to the individual, or family scripts. Cultural scripts might be influential in ways that are not known when a person is 'inside' their own culture. This importance may emerge when a learner meets a new culture.

We have not been judging some scripts as 'good' and others as less significant. There is no one way of being an effective learner and much depends on the features of the context one encounters. What happens in new contexts? How do learners with different scripts interpret the experiences they meet? Before looking at some evidence on this, we suggest an overarching theme for Chapter 1: the variety of views about learning.

A theme: conceptions of learning

Cultural scripts are always about something, and this book examines cultural scripts for learning. Among the varieties and differences that have been identified, it is also possible to see a difference in how the very focus of learning is conceived. There are varying conceptions of learning (Marton *et al.*, 1993) which inform the scripts, and have implications for the roles and activities in learning. The data in the empirical study discussed in this book throw light on three major conceptions of learning.

a. The receptive conception

> In Italy the lessons are very dense in content . . . the lessons are two-hour intense lessons. We sit down and listen for two hours without disturbing (Anita, Italy).

Many learners see learning as a novice receiving from an expert teacher. In this view knowledge is an accurate heap of facts that can be reproduced. Learners succeed by listening to the teacher, who is supposed to provide the learners with the truth about the world, reading for the author's point of view and reproducing the knowledge received from listening and reading. Students with this conception expect the teachers to be active in supplying notes, providing answers to their questions and directing them with clear instructions in relation to writing assignments. Consequently, they limit their own responsibilities as learners.

b. The constructivist conception

In this view learning is an active process, through which humans come to know their world and make sense of experience, and this process often takes place through human beings interacting and sharing meanings with each other.

Learners with a constructivist conception of learning seem to engage actively in the process of learning, and also reflect using metacognitive skills. They appear to embrace alternative stories of coming to know and are capable of making choices of opinion from different versions of the truth.

c. The mixed conception of learning

Some students made comments which called upon elements of both conceptions. At times this was because their view of learning seemed to be different in different situations. They might see learning as reception while in a teaching session, but see learning as construction while they studied alone. Perhaps for some of these their full range of learning strategies was not therefore available to them in all situations.

These important differences emphasise the larger point that learning is not a socially and culturally isolated act but is always embedded in the cultural–social components of any culture. The idea of learning, what is knowledge and how it is constructed vary significantly across different cultures.

Again, we do not intend these conceptions to be seen as rigid categories. Rather, they pick up broad themes which have been identified in the cultural scripts that learners talked about as relating to their home contexts. Some learners gave evidence that their own conceptions began to change as they met a new context. After time, some learners with a receptive conception of learning appeared to move on to a constructivist conception or to a mixed conception of learning, taking responsibility to different degrees for their own learning.

So now we move to consider more about the experiences of learners coming to the UK, when they meet teaching and learning occasions which seem to operate from a different script.

2 Homesick: learning sick?

In Chapter 1 we aimed to highlight variety in cultural interpretations for the various activities and relationships that are involved in approaches to learning. Among that variety we do not intend to imply any judgement of better or worse, for the evidence shows that there is no simple 'winner' either in processes or outcomes of learning across widely differing cultures (Watkins, 2000).

We aim to consider what happens when such a variety of cultural scripts come together in the context of learning in higher education. How do different cultural ways of understanding the activities and relationships for learning co-exist? What happens if learners who come from different cultures to learn in British universities do not share similar narratives of learning to those that are embodied in the host universities in the UK?

Learning in a university which is not in one's home country can be an experience of encountering difference, but what is that experience like? What does it feel like? How do learners make sense of it? Theoretically at least, it could be a smooth and constructive experience. Alternatively, it might be one of contradiction and shock.

In this chapter we aim to point out how learners from various cultures make sense of the actions and meanings related to the process of learning as they understand and experience it during their sojourn in the contexts of learning in their host universities.

Talking or shouting?

Differing views regarding the role and purpose of talk in learning, together with the roles implied, are highlighted very early.

> Believe me, the first day, I was shocked to find out how the classroom works here. My God, I was waiting, waiting and waiting. Where is the lecture? What is this? Why are the students shouting this much? Why the teacher is listening to the students while it should be the other way? . . . Actually, I was thinking how I can learn for a MA degree in this manner (Raju, Malaysia).

The experience of meeting difference can be one of surprise and perhaps one of shock, but crucially it may lead learners to question whether they can learn.

The view 'it's the teacher's job to talk' emerges again, but this time as a result of its felt absence:

> The other bit is that . . . I am a full-time student and I have only two days of classes for two days of the week. I was very scared. And during these two classes there was nothing much . . . no learning as such. Just arguments over this and that. Some times, just stupid arguments. . . . You see. I phoned someone back home and told about this and he asked me 'Oooo, wh...aaat? What are you going to learn like this?' (Oliver, Malawi).

So not only might the experience of different cultural scripts be uncomfortable, but it might also lead to judgements of the others one meets, as indicated here when describing peers as 'shouting' and engaged in 'stupid' arguments.

> Why can not they let us listen to the teacher? . . . No lecture . . . it is all talking, discussing, arguing with each other . . . it is going mad. . . . All the students talk all the time (John, Kenya).

These judgements about the form of talk in classrooms should not be taken to mean that the learners making such judgements are not interested in taking a critical stance; quite the opposite in some cases. For instance, learners from Fiji, Japan and India mentioned that even though they were not happy with talk in the classroom, they are critical when involved in writing and thinking. In some cultures, criticality is not to be shown in spoken contributions: it is addressed more quietly, in private.

Others felt comfortable with critical talk in the classroom, but regarded the discussions they experienced as commonplace talk, to the point of not learning:

> My God, I was scared of everything. Everything was strange. I am not used to this silly way of shouting in the class. . . . I mean this pub way of discussing . . . these discussions can happen anywhere and not up to the level to occur inside a classroom in an institute like this . . . . Nothing learnt at the end of the lesson (Anita, Italy).

Clearly this comment highlights an issue about the style of discussion, which is necessary for group conversations to promote effective learning, but the feelings generated when this is a strange experience may lead someone to say they have not learnt.

Learning from one another, or learning from one other?

Learning and teaching in groups was a recurring approach in the host university studied, and it became important to analyse this in terms of power dynamics among the student groups, especially in terms of the power in fluency of English language:

> When I was doing my MA here I had a very frustrating experience. We come here to learn after sacrificing so many things and when you find that you are here to listen to some irrelevant stories continuously told by those who are fluent in English, it is very frustrating. . . . There was a gentleman . . . he was dominating and almost controlling the class. Just talking, telling his experience which is not important to us, and taking all the time. This happened all the time. And surprisingly, the teacher let it happen without any interference. Never thought that others are there to learn.

> I learnt nothing from that particular module. I think that lessons
> should be planned so that every learner gets a chance to learn
> (Roger, Ghana).

Again, this comment highlights something important about issues of dominance in a group which is aiming to learn, but the feelings of frustration and a view of oneself as less fluent in English may again lead learners to feel disempowered in this strange situation:

> International students . . . their voices are not heard and they are not
> happy and feeling comfortable . . . it is always the English talking . . .
> you know, it is their language . . . from the childhood, they get used
> to this talking and arguing thing. So they talk all the time. No space
> for others. . . . You know, in our culture, we have a different style of
> talking . . . the group discussion thing is often a waste of time for us
> (Zeema, Brazil).

Thus, learners mention how the dominance of one particular group, which has English language fluency, can influence others' experience of learning. Such views highlight how some learners become privileged and empowered, while others feel dislocated within certain teaching–learning situations.

Writing or conforming?

Responses to encountering a different culture for going about writing were not so instant as those for talk; perhaps this is because writing experiences came a little later than the first day! But some learners found that the conventions of academic writing were not easy to accept in a neutral manner:

> Here . . . every statement is been referred to, and even when you
> read something you get disturbed [by references in the text].
> Definitely tooo much. Back home we express things in a better way
> . . . any reader can understand. Here, whatever you write you need

to refer it to the writer. Otherwise they call it something. Pagaa...ism? I was very angry about this (Kengi, Kenya).

In addition, the new convention for writing is seen to reflect the local cultural script rather than some universal criterion, and as a result is felt to devalue one's home culture. Some learners felt their voice as a writer was now more confused.

> Now see, whatever I write is my own and not my own. Because my writing is influenced by what I read, listen to and talk with other people. So, how am I going to give reference to all what I write? . . . You know . . . these individualistic . . . societies . . . every single thing has an owner. Very different from us (Kengi, Kenya).

> When I write, I go on talking about general things without giving reasons or evidence . . . I just go round and round without going to the point concretely. But . . . learning to write in the way they do it here is difficult since it is very different from how we write (Marina, Mexico).

For other learners, what seemed to be different conventions in writing, and how they were offered, led to feelings of dislocation, disempowerment and:

> I was taken to be an expert of English language back home. But now, I am told to do like this and that and the language seems to turn the other way round. Now I feel I do not know any English . . . I do not know anything (John, Kenya).

> It is not prescribed there [in Malawi], in terms of doing what. I have been using English for years, as a person with a title in our ministry. Never felt inhibited or anything. I knew I know the language. When I was sent the paper to write a critique about . . . for my qualifying essay . . . they sent me from A to Z . . . they went on to say . . . you make sure you have quoted others and put them in the bibliography . . . as if I have never been to school. I felt it. Why send all these details? I know how to review an article. You know, this is how they teach us to write in their way (Oliver, Malawi).

Such comments highlight how some learners read the conventions of writing as advocated by the host university, when they are given to them as mere rules to follow. It implies that what is appreciated as academic writing in a particular culture of learning is not necessarily valued as significant by learners who come from cultures with different scripts for writing in academe. It further suggests that an encounter of different scripts for learning can be interpreted in multiple ways.

After some time, some learners began to question the apparent authority for the writing conventions they were given, especially if these had not been explained and warranted.

> Because they have written a lot, done a lot of research, they have the authority in writing. Everything is in their point of view . . . you see what ever method of writing, or learning we use is not taken as important. They do not say why their ways are better even. We are just asked to follow them. . . . At the beginning I thought this is a better way of writing. But now it is not better . . . not apt for me . . . may be for the English context (Yasin, Taiwan).

They thus questioned the applicability of these approaches in their home context, thereby raising doubts about the nature of international education. In the meantime, the learners appear to build up their own understandings in relation to issues such as *who* constructs *what* knowledge, as well as *which* knowledge came to be the globally accepted knowledge.

Reading or labouring?

At some level, the act of reading is something in which all students will be accomplished. But in their new context they may meet new purposes and strategies for going about reading. And it does not follow that these new approaches will be accepted or indeed that they will be viewed as valuable.

> Learning to read as they want is difficult for me. It takes time to
> learn all these. I do not know. . . . Even to write also we have to read
> a lot (Magi, France).

For some learners therefore, it may be that meeting new approaches
disrupts the competences they bring. Whether such disruption is a
temporary matter is an open question.

Other learners questioned the degree to which critical reading was
a viable strategy for them to apply back in their own culture:

> In my country, there is no culture of reading. There is a scarcity of
> resources for reading and our people are not much for reading. In
> the university, there is only one book on a particular topic and the
> teacher takes it to teach all the students. So, we listen and take
> down notes. . . . There is nothing called critical reading for learning.
> When there are no books how can we read critically or in what ever
> ways? . . . I mean this scanning and critical reading . . . and this and
> that is not going to work there . . . I don't know, it is not easy for me
> to learn the way they do it here . . . and even if learn it with much
> difficulty . . . for what? (Donald, Uganda).

Such comments raise questions regarding issues of the universal
applicability of any approaches to reading for learning or, in general,
for learning. It also highlights that different cultural scripts for reading
which are very much context-bound cannot be easily abandoned or
adapted merely because the learners enter a new context of learning.

No teaching no learning?

If teachers in a new context do not behave in ways which make sense
according to the cultural scripts that learners bring, some learners feel
they cannot go about their learning in a way that is meaningful to
them.

> Here, they all the time emphasise self-learning and self-directed
> learning. But how can we learn when there is no direction at all?
> When we finish learning some subjects, we find that we have learnt

nothing. . . . I still find it difficult to learn without proper guidance or input from the teacher (Akihiro, Japan).

If the role of the teacher functions in a way that is seen as 'lack of input', these learners seem to wait for the teachers to teach them. The contradiction which the learners experience may be mirrored in their judging of teachers as displaying contradictions:

The teachers here show as if they know everything. Anyway, I think they are not even prepared for the lesson. You ask them a question, without any shame they will just say 'I don't know'. That is terrible. The teachers in this university believe that learning takes place inside those noisy classrooms and they do not teach anything and I feel it is very wrong . . . I thought I was going to learn a lot here . . . but . . . (Kengi, Kenya).

The style of judgements which are made of teachers highlights cultural scripts, and what happens if a new experience does not match them:

Another thing I am disappointed is that the teachers here . . . they never teach. Back home, at the end of the lesson, we have something to take home with us. But here . . . nothing. You ask a question . . . any time they will say, in front of the whole class that they do not know the answer. Our teachers, even the school teachers will never do that . . . and look at their lessons. For me it is like . . . anything is alright. Teachers are not well organised. They say something, put something on the OHP . . . that is the lesson. No clear objectives I think (Magi, France).

Some also make judgements of the act of teaching that they encounter in the host university in terms of the 'quality' the learners attach to the act of teaching, which is shaped by their familiar cultural script for teaching:

I found that just going to the class does not make sense here. You just get lost. . . . What teachers and the other students say make no sense at all. . . . You see . . . no quality. . . . We have some online projects to do. I read some of the answers written by other students . . . my God . . . it is a different culture here. Anything is accepted as an answer. Back home we have a structure, we can not write just any rubbish in an academic answer. But goodness . . . here . . . teachers are not bothered about the quality (Gifti, Jamaica).

After time, learners may later adopt a critical stance and highlight contradictions between the stated approach to teaching and their experience of it:

one thing interesting is that they say it is learner-centred. And complain that students like us are passive . . . we just listen. But the thing is we learn in English and the teachers just let the native students dominate the class discussions or what ever it is. We are not that fast in talking. . . . Even if we want to say something, no time or space. It is only those who can talk will talk all the time. Teachers are not bothered who learns what. So, where is their learner-centred way? We are made to listen to the native students (Freeda, Cyprus).

Even though they say that these universities are very much learner–centred it does not really happen. . . . Here, the teachers did not understand me and I did not understand them. When we come here, the teachers think that we will understand their ways of doing things within one minute (Pamela, Finland).

But Freeda also has some positive experiences.

Anyway, this depends on the teacher. In my [name of teacher] lessons, everybody gets a chance . . . lessons are not just going. . . . He plans it well and we all learn there.

The argument here is that even though their host university is said to promote self-directed learning, the actual, practical issue in relation to pedagogic situations is that often the native learners dominate the lessons since the teachers do not plan and organise the lessons for effective distributed learning. Consequently, learners who are less fluent in English listen rather than actively participate.

Informal teachers, or is it a mask?

Writers on teacher–student relationships in multicultural contexts of higher education (for example, Todd, 1997) suggest that learners who come to western universities from other cultures are not used to informal, friendly teachers. However, some learners in this study took a different view, judging their teachers as passive, formal, or unauthentic.

> Here, the teacher is as passive as the teacher in our culture. She is always sitting down and reading some notes from a book and never looks at any of us. Very boring (Freeda, Cyprus).

Such comments raise questions about the assumptions held about the role of the teacher in certain parts of the world.

> Even though they pretend to be informal, they are formal . . . teachers are more superficial here. They do these fancy moving around the class . . . letting the students shout. . . . But they are very formal, like the same, old Italian teacher (Anita, Italy).

> Here, the people are blank . . . the teachers are animated in the classrooms. . . . It is a programmed way of showing humour . . . they have the mask on . . . not laughing in the heart . . . the kind of engagement is not frank (Lee, Hong-Kong).

Again, contrary to the view found in the literature and elsewhere that learners from other cultures can be passive and non-interactive, these learners took a critical stance on their situation. Some students from cultures that are sometimes associated with 'formal' teacher–student relations were among those who were critical of their teachers for being formal.

Such students relate the role of the teacher in British universities with the commercial and institutional values that are intertwined with their roles, contrasting the sort of exchange that is about learning with the sort of exchange that is about finance.

> They are not friendly and approachable. . . . They show as if they are
> very helpful and highly approachable. O...h . . . not at all. Teach you
> something and gone. . . . To maintain a good relationship you need
> to exchange information. Here the teachers are not that. You just
> pay, pay and pay and be gone. (Seema, Brazil).

On some occasions, the teacher–student relationship that learners
experience in the host university is described with emotions:

> The teachers here are very strange and different. . . . In these classes
> you are very invisible and I could not talk anything and got bored.
> . . . The teachers even never look at you. They will not see the . . . girl
> sitting in a corner. They don't notice you. You come and sit down in a
> corner. . . . Only one gender lecturer was nice to me. . . .
>
> And the teachers were not very inviting. They will always go with those
> who are always talking, and who can talk fast . . . may be they talk sense or
> nonsense . . . and yes, they talk about interaction . . . no, it never happens
> with some learners (Meesha, Sudan).

Thus, some question the idea of the interactive, informal teacher
who is said to exist in the host university culture.

Peer interaction or peer separation?

The dimension of classroom situations which focused on peers and peer
interaction was also one where judgements emerged. Some learners
with differing cultural scripts offered views on the behaviour of their
peer learners, and by implication affected the peer relationships
emerging between learners.

Some seemed to agree with the principle of peer interaction to
support learning, but described the native students in their host culture
as not behaving in a way which would promote it. Again judgements
of contradiction were made.

> I do not like it. They would never ever want to share any view with us who are not English. They will go on shouting in the class. But never with us. Very distant kind of learners. . . . And you know, these are the people who write and talk about interactive learning and this and that (Stella, Bulgaria).

The distance between the native students in the host learning culture is seen as a disadvantage in terms of learning through interaction:

> I did not know even whether they looked at me or not. . . . The English, they always maintain a distance from you. . . . So you cannot exchange any learning experience or what ever with them. . . . And you know, it is always easy to make friends with the Asians . . . they are friendly and helpful . . . I have made two friends, one from Japan, the other from Malaysia . . . we discuss assignments . . . very helpful (John, Kenya).

> Back home, definitely there is more interaction among learners for learning, since we need to do things on our own. We have to talk with the friends and come to conclusions and write assignments. And I think we learn more like this . . . by discussing with friends. . . . But when you come here, more often, learning is your own business, kind of isolated . . . very few chances to learn from others (Jordan, Nigeria).

It is very important to note that some of the same voices that were explaining why there was little point for discussion in the classroom say that they learn more by discussing with friends – but in another context, that is, outside the classroom. We do not see this as evidence of a mixed conception, but evidence for the important way in which scripts relate to contexts. As contexts are strongly defined by the actors who are to be found in them, the classroom with the teacher has a very different set of meanings and actions from another context without the teacher but with peers.

This point invites us to think about learners in a range of contexts – their learning landscape if you will – and to consider the idea that the range of spaces available for learning could be seen in markedly different ways for different cultures. Some learners might emphasise the classroom as a space for their active engagement, whereas other learners might do the exact opposite. We will consider some possible implications of this in the next chapter, after considering the overall picture of the first two chapters.

So?

In this chapter, a recurring theme which may seem obvious but which is worth stating is that learners with varying cultural scripts tend to read the new situation through their own cultural scripts for learning. This may seem commonplace, but the emotions associated with such a reading are not: they can include feeling shocked, disempowered, stuck, dislocated, devalued and misjudged. And the impact of such emotions may well be linked to the evidence that learners may question whether they can learn at all in the new context.

We have no evidence that any teachers would want the experience of their learners to be characterised by such emotions and responses. Many would perhaps be shocked in their turn. But this issue is made more difficult for teachers to hear about and therefore to play a part in resolving by the fact that learners from other cultures may distance themselves from communicating this to their peers and teachers, again for a host of cultural reasons. Hence some of the feelings of alienation and disappointment are unlikely to be heard by teachers.

With time, rather than embracing the unfamiliar without complication, some learners come to question the situation in which they find themselves. Here the English language through which knowledge is constructed in UK institutions is a key focus: learners whose first language is not English feel that it privileges some participants, while excluding some others. Some learners spoke in very emotional terms about this issue.

The central issue emerging from the experience of learners with different cultural scripts for learning is that of communication. If their experience in a UK university is not in accord with their previous experience, a communication gap sometimes arises. We find the analysis of this as a communication gap important, because it signals constructive action which could be taken for a situation that is about a gap in perceptions. Other sorts of analyses might lead to less constructive possibilities: for example, the idea of a 'clash in perceptions' could be hazardous, since it might sustain the idea of a 'blame game' emerging between teachers and students, in which the teachers view some students as 'passive' and the students view some teachers as 'disorganised'. Unfortunately, some of the literature on the experience of learners from other cultures could be read in this way.

Learners are not likely to embrace new scripts for learning merely because they have changed their context for learning for a time. This seems especially likely if they are given no rationale for another way. Instead, they tend to preserve their own scripts for learning, at the same time as critically viewing their new encounter of learning.

This situation calls for a more explicit communication about the very focus of everyone's activity in the context concerned: that focus is teaching and learning.

A theme: conceptions of teaching

The study on which this book is based has its starting focus in cultural scripts for learning, but it is perhaps not surprising for a study that is based in formal learning organisations that this should soon link to cultural scripts for teaching.

Numerous studies of teaching and learning in higher education around the world have identified different conceptions of teaching (for example, Samuelowicz and Bain, 2001). These studies have often identified three broad types which reflect different positions on a number of underlying dimensions.

a. The transmission conception

This conception of teaching is mainly teacher-centred, and is focused on transmission of content (imparting knowledge or information). It is sometimes more likely to be found in course environments where teachers are valued for their specialist knowledge, and therefore exercise control over what is taught, and assessment is broadly that of asking students to reproduce such knowledge.

b. The 'changing understandings' conception

This conception is mainly learner-centred, and is focused on students' understandings and the need sometimes to change their conceptions of the subject matter, through a process whereby the teacher supports students' learning. It is sometimes more likely to be found in course environments where student learning and application is valued, and teachers are expert in facilitating the learning process, and in which assessment is more likely to ask students to apply knowledge.

c. The mixed conception

In many studies, a number of respondents also describe views of teaching which contain elements of both of the above, and on these occasions they often describe features of the environment and a range of pressures or tensions as reasons for the mixed state of affairs.

In this study, learners themselves described such tensions in contexts they knew, especially those in a formal institution of learning:

> Back home, learner is more liberal and they can question and argue with the teacher. . . . We have an approach similar to [name of teacher in the UK university] in our country. But . . . a young teacher had once tried to use it and there was much criticism about it. Sometimes, we still like to complete the syllabus rather than worrying about active learning (Veronica, Austria).

This quotation suggests a tension even when the home culture seems to support a constructivist conception of learning; when it comes to classroom teaching, 'practical' considerations and ideas like 'completing the syllabus' may bring out a transmission conception of teaching.

Whose conception of teaching?

The outline offered above has deliberately introduced the different conceptions of teaching without specifying whose conceptions they are. Most studies have focused on teachers' conceptions of teaching, and only a few on students' conceptions.

But many of the experiences of learners from other cultures that underlie this book can usefully be thought of in terms of a gap existing between learners' conception of teaching and teachers' conception of teaching. This gap is not always in the direction that some stereotypes of overseas learners might suggest (Kember, 2000). For example, students like Seema may have a constructivist view of learning, and a conception of teaching which focuses on teachers engaging with students' questions and promoting extended dialogue. With this view she evaluates her experience critically:

> You know, I tried to talk with them from the beginning, since I like to get to know them and learn things. But very rarely they would ask you back about yourself. They will never want to continue any kind of long conversation with you. . . . They were never interested in me as a student or in my questions (Seema, Brazil).

So learners who view learning as an active process and seek a 'changing conceptions' view of teaching may find fault in their experience of their host university if there is a lack of opportunity to be interactive for the purpose of learning.

We conclude this chapter with thoughts about the 'match' or otherwise between teachers' and learners' conceptions of teaching. Simplifying the conceptions of learning into the two poles of the dimension, and plotting the teachers' conception against the learners' conception gives the four main cells of the diagram below.

		Learners' conception of teaching	
		Transmission	Changing understanding
Teachers' conception of teaching	Transmission	Match is good Quality of learning is impaired	Some mismatch Learners adapt to the teacher's view
	Changing understanding	Mismatch Some learners adapt to the teacher's view	Match is good Quality of learning is high

Figure 2.1 Learners' and teachers' conceptions of learning

This diagram attempts to capture some of the voices of learners in this study, as well as findings from other research (Campbell *et al.*, 2001, Kember, 2001). In particular it captures findings from universities as well as schools, which indicate that:

- Students' approaches to learning are influenced by their (cultural) conceptions of learning and their reading of the learning environment.

- Teachers' approaches to teaching are influenced by their (cultural) conceptions of teaching and their reading of the teaching environment.

- When teachers adopt surface transmission approaches to teaching, nearly all students respond with surface reception approaches to learning.

- When teachers adopt deeper understanding approaches to teaching, some students (those with a more constructivist initial view of learning) respond with deeper approaches to learning.

- Students' deeper approaches to learning are associated with higher quality learning outcomes.

The value of this idea is that the communication gap which has been identified in the students' experiences reported here could now start to be seen as a communication gap over a key focus: the process of teaching and learning.

Some of the evidence summarised above is helpful when starting to ask the questions that will be addressed in Chapter 3, for example:

- How may teaching be organised so as to hear, recognise and accommodate different cultural scripts for learning?

- How may teaching be organised so that more students can achieve deeper approaches to learning and the higher quality learning outcomes?

Already these questions may reflect an intercultural stance, not merely a multicultural one. So we will consider ways through which all cultures may learn with and about each other, rather than limit ourselves to the dominant assumption that other cultures should adapt to UK cultural norms. Notions such as 'assimilation' and 'adjustment' are inadequate to address the picture we have described from the evidence.

3   How about an intercultural home?

If higher education seeks to avoid the situation where learners from other cultures have experiences like those described in the previous chapter, then a range of things may be candidates for change. But in a context where communication is not effective, any talk about change can generate defensiveness, or even another 'blame game'. Indeed it could be argued that talk of such learners needing to 'assimilate' is an example of blaming the victim.

So we start this chapter with an explicit questioning of whose role it is to change, in order to recognise change in both parties; and the need for this to be achieved if the situation itself is to change.

Whose change?

This book has highlighted some of the responses which may ensue when learners from other cultures meet a new context. But such an account should not be taken to suggest that learners from other cultures do not recognise key cultural issues, or understand themselves to be handling a changed cultural context:

> I tried to adapt to the surprise. . . . It is important for me to survive here as a student and as a human being. . . . We need to do what Romans do while in Rome . . . not a lifelong change . . . just for the time being (Saman, Sri Lanka).

Notably Saman indicates that such a change may be temporary and particular to the context.

Other learners had explicitly considered any 'need to change' and had adopted a selective stance, again based on their understanding of context differences:

> Maybe I try to get used to certain things which I feel important. You see . . . not all what they say and do will apply back home. So, I don't want to follow for no reason. I will choose what is important for me personally and to my work and take only those things home . . . and I do not think we need to change everything merely because we come here to learn (Jordan, Nigeria).

This highlights the way in which learners can hold different views about *why* and to *which degree* they should change – if they want to change as learners. The strategic nature of their choice has been highlighted in other research (Kettle, 2005) as an important aspect of creating agency and identity for international students.

Yet other learners have anticipated the multicultural context they are joining, and its power dynamics, and this has led them to adopt a proactive purposeful stance:

> to prove ourselves to these people. Because these people always look down upon the learners who come from non-western countries . . . we need to tell them we have something important to tell. . . . The British think 'What can we learn from Africans? Indians? We know. . . . We know'. We have the responsibility to represent our country to say that our country has something wealthy to say (Pat, South Africa).

Further still, some of the respondents quoted in this book have described how they became more of the type of learner which they judged appropriate for a UK university ('a western learner', in one respondent's view).

There were a few occasions when learners talked about their experience of learning in the new learning context as a constructive experience and mentioned their desire to change into the new way of approaching learning. The desire for change had been encouraged by a particular teacher and his ways of facilitating the learning process.

> You know, I learn more from [name of teacher]'s classes than from other classes definitely. I think his classes and his way of teaching is a good example for someone to take and put in her or his learning script (Freeda, Cyprus).

This example also illustrates that the scripts for teaching were not uniform in the institution where the study took place.

For others, change as a learner was slow and remained difficult:

> I am not used to talking during the lesson. Not trained to that. . . . But now . . . I have to talk and learn which is very difficult for me to do. Alternatives are there for everything. (but) When I am in conversation with my supervisor, I still ask 'what is the correct answer for this?' . . . So, I am not for arguing for alternatives even after studying four years in this Institute (Ameena, Maldives).

But the point remains: this learner was making changes. Again, these examples emphasise that learners from other cultures will never simply jettison their home culture and adopt another. Rather, they live at various shifting points in between their native narratives and the novel narratives told in the new learning experience. But a recurring message is that their teachers and tutors may not get to hear about this.

Teachers too have made a range of adaptations, some of them informed by a wish to develop a more student-centred environment. Their direct voice on change is not available here since they were not respondents in the study on which this book is based. So we cannot assess the degree to which their changes depart from their own cultural scripts.

But some learners indicated that they thought change was on the agenda for teachers as well as for learners:

> I think the teachers should accommodate the other students in a
> way, I mean . . . as they are . . . I do not think the teachers here ever
> pay attention that some have different views and experience of
> learning . . . just go on doing what they do. . . . We use different
> languages. . . . Here, we are using their language to understand
> them and their teaching (John, Kenya).

Within an international market of higher education, many people
have a critical stance on the effects of globalisation. In all probability
teachers would embrace the idea that the act of learning should not
be viewed according to one dominant story constructed by institutions
in particular parts of the world. So the issue becomes: how must practice change for this to be achieved?

Pay attention to the learning experience

One of the key messages from listening to the learning experiences of
learners who come from different cultures is that their stories give
evidence of them bringing considerable commitment, coping with
substantial difficulty and finding new ways through difficult territory
at times. So paying attention to their experience pays off for the host
institution's understanding; the pay-off could become even greater for
all – teachers and peer learners – if reviews of the learning experience
are to become a greater part of the course experience.

Just as in other sectors of education, the dominant discourse in
a course is often about teaching and assessment. So the process of
learning, through which people achieve their goals, is not heard and
their best hopes for learning may become distorted or discarded:

> For me learning is a process. Here, they say yes, it is so. But, see: it is
> 'taught masters'. . . . At the end of the day, teachers can fail you in
> the course. No matter learning is a process for you or not. . . . It is
> their assessment which decides whether your learning is good or
> bad. . . . We don't eat properly, don't sleep properly. . . . For what?
> To finish the assignment – to get the grade. . . . For me this is not
> learning (Lee, Hong Kong).

Developing more of a focus on learning and the learning experience will be assisted by two important strands:

- review of the concept of learning in the host institution
- reshaping the ways of teaching to improve learning.

Reviewing concepts of learning

The act of learning does not have a singular meaning across cultures. Within teaching–learning contexts, where there is an encounter of multiple cultures, the concept of learning cannot simply be understood as according with the dominant concepts of learning. The points below attempt to explain a richer view.

Learning as a set of interactions

The act of learning cannot be satisfactorily viewed as passing on new knowledge from the teacher to the learner. Learners do not embark as vacuums on the journey of learning. They join a situation of teaching–learning with their experiences of prior knowledge. Learning is an interactive process between what the learners already know and what they are going to co-construct in another learning encounter. The interactive journey of learning is also shaped and influenced by the relationships between teacher and student as well as between the peer learners:

> I learn more by discussing and listening to different ideas of peers.
> I learn more (Freeda, Cyprus).

Thus, learning is an outcome of a network of relationships and interactions – intellectual and social at the same time. It reflects what learners already know and what they are going to construct and co-construct in the new learning environment. When that environment also includes learners and teachers who come from diverse cultures of learning, the sets of possible interactions become richer and the possibilities for learning greater.

But a pitfall would be to focus only on interactions in the classroom. We need to make sense of learners as human beings with lives outside of the institutions of learning. If we reconsider the idea that learning occurs only within the four walls of the classroom, new opportunities arise for foregrounding interactions elsewhere in their landscape of learning. Anyone who is new to a country may feel strange and may value affiliation with those who feel similar. So informal groups of peers are important spaces, and if the learning relations there are not dominated by the presence of teachers they can be supportive of learning and achievement.

Coming to know as a cultural process

Learning does not occur within a cultural–social vacuum. Hence, what is knowledge, how it is constructed and communicated, varies across cultures. What is accepted as the commonly used cultural script for talking for learning in one culture may be rejected in another culture of learning as passive and non-constructive. The significant message conveyed through such cultural differences is that what is accepted and valued as 'knowledge' does not relate to universals. Hence, the process of coming to know as well as knowing which is valued within the host university may not be readily embraced by learners who come from diverse cultures of learning. Instead of embracing the new, the learners will take their own time to understand the different spaces in the new landscape. They may be selective about the narratives of knowing constructed by the host learning culture, judging some as significant or valuable, often for their applicability in a different culture.

Hence, the culturally embedded nature of learning invites teachers to be reflexive about the process of learning. It also encourages them to rethink.

- It will not be possible to make sense of everyone's learning through the dominant views of learning.

- Assumptions made about some learners will be inappropriate, so are worthy of review and inquiry.

- A culturally diverse context of teaching and learning requires the development of approaches, which help the full range of learners to feel included.

Reshaping teaching to promote inclusive learning

If different cultures create different varieties of how we go about learning, and these are not simple to jettison, a context of international higher education could respond by making sense of learning as a process of change, a journey through new landscapes of learning to identify and construct one's own territories of knowing. Within this process, learners may engage in choosing, embracing, adjusting and rejecting particular knowledge and ways of knowing. More rejections would imply less learning. It may result in learners feeling alien in the new context of learning. In contrast to the feeling of alienation, a feeling of inclusiveness improves the experience of learning.

With these understandings in mind, it becomes possible to develop greater cultural appropriacy in teaching, content outcome and communication. Some possibilities are proposed below.

Being open-handed: cultural issues in approaches to teaching

A major concern of some respondents in the study on which this book is based is 'why one should follow' the host ways of doing learning.

> I have a difficulty in writing here. . . . Jee...sus, since I started writing, I am asking myself 'so do I really know English'? . . . And I am still thinking, so.oo, what is wrong with the English I use? (Gifti, Jamaica).

If an institution presents ways of approaching learning as rules, this will not contribute to an inclusive learning and teaching environment.

Teachers need to be open-handed about the ways of going about teaching and learning that are promoted. This entails offering reasons for the approaches which are taken rather than not mentioning them or enforcing them as rules. For example, if discussion approaches are used, there is a need to explain and discuss what such approaches might offer and to invite participants to review how they best operate. When new conventions in writing are introduced these need to be explained, not merely told. If 'critical thinking' is encouraged, the rationale, history and interpersonal ethics of this need attention. Otherwise, it is difficult to prevent some learners from feeling that they are not making sense of the new learning culture:

> If you do not give yourself time to think how things happen here, you can get lost . . . I think there should be an opportunity at the beginning or before you come in . . . you need to communicate these things. But they do not do it in the inauguration. Just eating crisps and drinking wine. If they make us aware that this is the way they go about learning here and give us some hints (Oliver, Malawi).

Being open-handed about the host culture will not by itself lead to cultural appropriacy in the learning process, but the discussion which follows may make a significant contribution.

One course team drafted an opening statement on such matters for inclusion in the pre-course handbook (see Appendix). This hopes to communicate a recognition of diversity and as such is better than implying that people will be asked simply to imitate western ways of learning. A further example from Harvard (Behn, 2007) invites learners new to an executive programme to recognise that we all bring scripts to a new learning situation, but that there is great value to be gained from questioning the dominant script.

Am I a stranger? Cultural issues in content

Process and content interact, so it is also fruitful to review the content of the course in terms of its cultural origins and examples, in order to avoid an Anglocentric curriculum and to engage with other cultural contexts. An example from an education course makes the point:

> They always talk about the British schools, British higher education
> . . . British this and that. In my class, there are few natives and more
> international students. Still, nothing is about our contexts of
> learning. We come here to learn about other contexts as well, that is
> true, but the thing is it should be useful when we go back home
> (Gifti, Jamaica).

This example also highlights the link that learners make between the content of a course and the outcome for them, which is put in terms of their key purpose – the applicability of learning 'back home'. Even in a context of international recognition and standardisation of qualifications, home issues are salient. Learners accept the importance of knowing the global context, but will question the relevance of learning experiences that only highlight the local context of the host institution.

> We come here and learn the theories constructed by the West. . .
> never question the bad aspects of them or applicability for us (Rifca,
> Pakistan)

Reviewing the course content will contribute to preventing a situation where some students play the role of the dislocated stranger in a classroom where knowledge is only focused on the British context.

Can I take this learning home? Cultural issues in outcomes

Learning is about making meaningful connections and a learner will regularly seek to make connections between new experiences on a course and their existing knowledge. For learners from another culture this informs how they try to make sense of the content as well as the pedagogy in terms of relevance to their home context.

Ideas and practices do not transfer to another culture through simply exporting or cross-cultural borrowing. The social life of ideas as they travel between cultures is always of interest. Adaptation and interpretation are always present, and to recognise and address this will not only enhance overseas learners' skills after any course, but will also engage their motivation while on course.

Any lecturer could inquire of course members:

- How do you think these ideas will be received in your home context and culture?

- Does the journey through which you have connected here with these ideas offer you any possible ways of improving their reception at home?

Can I make sense of them? Cultural issues in communication

Communication is one of the major requirements for any learning to take place. The medium of instruction needs to be carefully used by teachers, since learners within an international context of learning have varying usages, pronunciation as well as differences in paralinguistic communication. For instance, most of the learners who use English as a second language use received pronunciation (RP) and standard English. And when teachers use regional accents, vocabularies specific to certain social classes or even paralinguistic communication such as gestures, language fillers (well . . . mmm . . . I mean . . .) instead of a more direct communication of ideas, some learners would find it difficult to make sense of language. This can directly influence their experience of learning:

> I think the tutors need to accommodate the new students in a way as they are. . . . We are using their language to understand them . . . I do not think that they ever pay attention that we are not native speakers. What if they happen to learn in our first language? They are so fast and cannot understand . . . we have a different dialect. . . . They never adjust their vocabulary. . . . It really hinders our progress in learning (John, Kenya).

So if there is a range of first languages among participants, it becomes possible for some of them to join up and process ideas in their first language and then relate their discussion to the whole class in English. Such support to their bilingualism may also support the development of an intercultural climate.

For teachers too, communication issues abound, but many communication issues are resolved through good communication.

- Ask, rather than assume.

- Listen to experience, rather than stereotype.

Communication that allows us to hear someone's real experience may help the deconstruction of some stereotyped views that may be held about learners and learning. It can also raise wider issues in a manageable way, such as global issues of who constructs knowledge, how it is articulated and transported globally, and which forms of knowledge are valued. Without such communication we increase the hazard identified in this study, of UK universities being seen as updated versions of imperialism in the global knowledge context. For instance:

> even if we want to speak, feel vulnerable. . . . It is this Black and White debate. Their language, White being the Masters . . . the Master's language. . . . It is only they who always talk (Rifca, Pakistan).

> We were colonised by the British . . . people were pointed at and got the work done. . . . No much freedom to argue. . . . Now, here we have to argue, be critical . . . all their rules, easy for them . . . rules always come from them . . . see . . . ee (Lee, Hong Kong).

But with communication, we not only open the possibility of making learning and teaching intellectually and interculturally enlightening processes, but also increase the chances of success with integrity in the international market for higher education.

To the extent that some of the suggestions made above lead to discussions which address matters of culture and learning, they will also mark a shift in multicultural contexts of higher education towards them becoming intercultural contexts.

Promote intercultural learning

The process of the research underlying this book – and hopefully the experience of reading it – fosters the possibility of seeing the different cultural scripts which learners bring as resources for enriching the process of teaching and learning. If we are able to embrace diversity as a resource (rather than view it as a problem) we may construct interculturally fluent pedagogies to address the needs of learners, as well as the global needs of higher education.

The descriptor 'multicultural' can all too often be a mere statement of fact – that multiple cultures exist within a context. 'Intercultural' can bring additional emphasis to a process of learning between people from varying cultures. When this process is effective, every culture may learn from every other, and every participant (including those from the host culture) may learn about their own culture.

The stance of this book could be seen as part of a discourse approach to intercultural learning (Scollon and Scollon, 1995), and our core concept of cultural scripts may provide extra practical value in such a stance. We think of intercultural fluency as the ability to engage with and relate to the stories of other cultures. This supports the art of crossing cultures (Storti, 1990) and crossing borders (Fennes and Hapgood, 1997). Intercultural fluency promotes increased degrees of understanding, extending from the low level, which is often about learning others' customs for instrumental purposes, to a higher level, which is to sense the rich meaning that informs lives in another culture.

Although some writers have complained about a lack of definition, the following captures important elements.

> Intercultural learning develops in learners the knowledge for
> recognising, valuing, and responding to linguistic and cultural

variability through processes of inferring, comparing, interpreting, discussing, and negotiating meaning. It extends beyond the development of declarative knowledge based on the presentation of cultural facts, and do's and don'ts in cross-cultural interactions.

Intercultural learning engages with all aspects of human 'knowing', communication and interaction. Going beyond 'cross-cultural education', intercultural learning requires not only observation, description, analysis, and interpretation of phenomena in the context of human communication and interaction, but also requires active participation in explaining, and thus understanding, human nature self-reflexively. This self-reflexive interaction in understanding human communication and its variable contexts of interaction is a dynamic, progressive process that engages teachers and learners in negotiating human interaction by reflecting on one's own intra- and intercultural identity.

Crichton *et al.*, 2004: 64

Intercultural learning does not just happen merely because classrooms are occupied by learners from diverse cultures. It can take place only when there is space for the interaction between teachers and learners. It can only happen when there are open spaces in an organisation within which learners and teachers can build up intercultural fluency so that they can find ways of affiliating with each other's narratives of learning. Hence, we highlight that the possibilities for intercultural learning in a particular educational organisation are largely shaped by the organisational culture. We identify two significant approaches to culture and learning that can exist in any educational organisation, which can influence intercultural learning:

- uniform view of culture and learning

- diverse views of culture and learning.

Organisations of education that display a *uniform view of culture and learning* may emphasise dominant stories about learning rather than inviting affiliation among diverse narratives of doing learning. Such an approach relies on assimilating and inducting all the learners to one specific way of going about learning. In organisations that operate with this approach, people may believe they have a 'culture-free' notion of learning, but this impossibility demonstrates that they have not learnt about their own culture and remain culture-bound rather than 'culture-free'.

Organisations that display *diverse views of culture and learning* may promote interaction among diverse cultures of learning and would expect that communication across cultures enriches the experience of learning. Within such an organisation, there will be more space for building up intercultural fluency. These spaces would offer teachers and learners contexts in which to exchange and articulate diverse values, feelings, meanings and viewpoints related to the experience of learning in a more constructive manner. Hence, the feeling of cultural alienation will be altered by active participation in learning and thereby improve the feeling that learning is the learner's own personal act.

Figure 3.1 offers a broad representation of the difference. Cultures (a) to (f) are represented, and the various arrows indicate the communication channels which are valued and promoted within the organisation. The difference between one-way and two-way arrows is crucial.

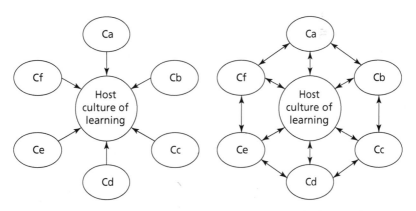

Uniformity view of culture and learning   Diversity view of culture and learning

Figure 3.1 Two possible approaches to the relation between culture and learning within an institution

We now move on to consider how we can promote intercultural fluency and then develop intercultural learning within spaces where diverse cultures of learning meet.

Invite communication

We are all cultural beings, yet if it were not for the existence of more than one culture we would not think about culture at all. So when it comes to activities which may promote intercultural learning, the key element is to invite communications which reveal both human similarity and cultural variation. Telling stories is a key vehicle (Bruner, 2002), and can be productive at many stages of a course experience. Course members can be invited to tell each other:

- the story of how you come to be on this course

- the story of what your previous course experiences were like

- the story of some surprising experiences during the early stages of your being here

- stories which describe the 'good teacher' and the 'good learner' in your culture of learning

- some stories of how other people from your country live their lives here, and so on.

A next step is to recognise and provide spaces for discussion of the ways that culture infuses the content, pedagogy and outcome of a course experience. This is not easy for anyone to do from 'within' their own culture, so help is needed. The presence of others with different scripts turns out to be an asset, through the twin processes of explaining and noticing. Learners can explain some of their cultural scripts through such things as their everyday idioms associated with learning, and descriptions of the contexts and processes they know well. Others can help by sharing what they notice about the different ways that different cultural groups approach their tasks for learning in a course context. With only a little practice, such discussions may become intercultural exchanges about learning experiences.

Encourage reflexivity

If we consider learning as a process, a journey, where the learners are encountering diverse landscapes of learning, such learning would definitely be supported and enriched by taking steps back and reflecting on the journey.

Teachers can encourage such reflection, for example, through the use of learning journals. These might record and reflect on past as well as current experiences of learning. They act as an important evidence base for development, and when used to review in groups can support a more equitable balance among the contributions of various voices. Learners and teachers can share understandings of where and why the experience of learning has been better or otherwise for learners. Teachers may also learn about situations where dominant narratives of learning have not contributed to enriching the experience of learning. For the learners, as they share their reflections and exchange views about learning, empathy and engagement can grow in a way which authentically enhances learners' understandings about each other.

Create open learning spaces for all

Any lack of opportunity for learners from other cultures to articulate their views can lead to feelings of isolation and dislocation. Such a situation creates cultural as well as pedagogic distance among learners and teachers, which again would discourage intercultural fluency.

> Something has to be done to promote good rapport among all the students and between teachers. . . . We need the opportunity to discuss (John, Kenya).

Group discussions can be a situation where learners voice their views, but they need to be orchestrated in a constructive way; otherwise cross-cultural judgements and interpretations will take the place of intercultural communication:

> They [students] just talk. They want to create an image that they know everything. They always have an answer even if it is incorrect . . . I do not know why they are doing that (Pat, South Africa).

At worst, if group contexts are not well orchestrated, experiences of intercultural conflict may arise:

> There was an incident. We were talking about something. I gave an example through my experience . . . this boy was telling that what I was telling was when it comes to personal experiences which experience is better. There is no better experience. So, when he said like that I got really angry because what I said was not rubbish. It does not mean that you cannot judge my experience through your experience. It also made me angry because the teacher did not want to discipline that boy. . . . He did not want to let the boy understand how I felt at that time (Pat, South Africa).

Such situations can be avoided. Structured group discussions in which learners are helped to prepare their contributions, exchange them in a structured way, develop new points from the exchange and then review the whole process will stand a good chance of success. By contrast unstructured group discussion can lead to feelings of chaos, increasing the possibility of culturally unexpected and unfamiliar experiences for all. The role of the teacher shifts from deliverer to orchestrator, someone who can help all learners to engage constructively with different ways of knowing.

Hence, open spaces where learners can story and negotiate diverse ways of knowing would promote greater affiliation and intercultural communication, and hence intercultural fluency. This in turn would help learners to interact, engage with or affiliate with other ways of coming to know with more confidence. This would also provide opportunities for learners to change within the process of walking through different learning landscapes and build up territories to address their own cultural–personal requirements for learning. Once learners reach this situation, they are not very far from experiencing an intercultural context of teaching and learning.

The emergence of intercultural learning spaces

Intercultural fluency, which is developed in a particular culture of learning, can be further improved into intercultural learning spaces. Spaces of learning in which learners as well as teachers can experience a new culture of learning, which results from the interaction among diverse learning cultures, including the dominant culture of learning, can be identified as intercultural spaces for learning. This particular space is distinctive from multicultural learning spaces in which we find only the presence of different cultures of learning. Instead, intercultural learning spaces are constructed as a result of the interaction among diverse ways of making knowledge. They shift from a more passive recognition of 'the world in this classroom' to the active creation of 'a new world in this classroom'. Therefore, it would be dominated neither by alternative ways of knowing nor by dominant ways of constructing knowledge. It would rather be a space in which multiple narratives of learning are accepted and expected as well as respected. Meanings of imperialism would be dissolved into sharing and exchanging diversity in learning as well as the agency of learners in their own learning. This particular learning context would be a dynamic space of hybrid learning in which learners could engage in learning in a novel manner. Hence, we call the learning experience one gains within an intercultural context of learning an enriched experience of learning.

Figure 3.2 indicates how an encounter of different cultures of learning can lead to the emergence of spaces of intercultural learning.

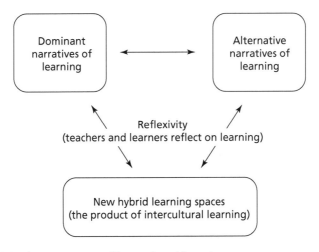

Figure 3.2 The emergence of intercultural learning spaces

As a result of the sorts of processes that have been briefly outlined in this chapter, we consider that there would be significant steps towards major goals.

- Any individual learner may be able to take a wider perspective on his or her learning.

- Group processes of communication may support increased intercultural acceptance.

- More people – in the host culture too – may become interculturally fluent.

If these possibilities are achieved, the best of the UK's historical contribution to education worldwide may be updated with integrity to a changed and changing world. To promote intercultural understanding and thereby enhance the process of learning in a multicultural context, as well as the transfer of learning from one cultural context to another, is an exciting and challenging goal for the international context.

Appendix: a draft statement by a teaching team

This example was drafted by a course team for inclusion in the handbook which course members receive before starting their course.

Occasionally some of our students tell us that the classes do not operate in ways they are used to, or that they had expected. Although they also tell us that the strangeness reduces as they come to understand the reasons, the points below might give you a sense of the culture in the classes, and help you over any initial surprise.

On our courses, course members are encouraged to discuss and to engage in dialogue. We encourage this because we know it develops the most powerful learning environments. As you come to see that there is a range of perspectives which are accepted as important to consider, you may come to feel more confident about contributing your own – and learning about it.

Your teachers have considerable experience and expertise, but they do not simply 'transmit' that to course members (whose role would then be a passive receiver). Rather their expertise is directed to promoting effective multi-way communication about the topic under consideration. Sometimes your teachers may say 'I don't know'.

On your course staff may operate in a way that is sometimes described as 'informal': they do not ask to be addressed formally; they engage in debate without losing face; they are treated more like peer professionals outside class. You are allowed (and sometimes even encouraged!) to take a view which is different from that of your teacher.

In your classes you may find yourself working in small groups, and the groupings may be changed over time to ensure that you meet a wide range of perspectives and have a chance to engage with them. We believe that different cultures are a resource for learning, and encourage you to do the same. We appreciate it when students help each other to learn.

For assignments you will be given scope to decide your topic and to find the path that accords with your own interests. This can feel strange at first, to the point that we find adult students asking their teachers what path they should follow.

Although everyone is studying to achieve an award, the staff do not spend a lot of time emphasising this or publicising grades, etc. This is because their emphasis is on the process of your learning (and that way we also find you get better grades!).

References

Atwood, J.D. (1996) *Family Scripts*. Chicago: Taylor and Francis.

Azuma. H. (2001) 'Moral scripts: A US–Japan comparison'. In H. Shimizu and R.A. LeVine (eds), *Japanese Frames of Mind: Cultural perspectives on human development*. Cambridge: Cambridge University Press.

Behn, R.D. (2007) *A New Learning Script*. Cambridge, MA: John F. Kennedy School of Government, Harvard University. [http://ksgexecprogram.harvard.edu/download/dgp/Learning.pdf]

British Council (2007) *Cultural Connections: Making the most of the international student experience*. London: British Council.

Bruner, J.S. (2002) *Making Stories*. New York: Farrar Straus and Giroux.

Campbell, J., Smith, D., Boulton-Lewis, G., Brownlee, J., Burnett, P.C., Carrington, S. and Purdie, N. (2001) 'Students' perceptions of teaching and learning: The influence of students' approaches to learning and teachers' approaches to teaching'. *Teachers and Teaching: Theory and Practice*, 7(2): 173–87.

Chan, V. (2001) 'Learning autonomously: the learners' perspectives'. *Journal of Further and Higher Education*, 25(3): 285–300.

Charmaz, K. (2000) 'Grounded theory: objectivist and constructivist methods'. In N.K. Denzin and Y.S. Lincoln (eds), *Handbook of Qualitative Research,* 2nd edn. Thousand Oaks, CA: Sage, pp. 509–35.

Cortazzi, M. and Jin, L. (1997) 'Communication for learning across cultures'. In D. MacNamara and R. Harris (eds), *Overseas Students in Higher Education: Issues in teaching and learning*. London: Routledge.

Crichton, J., Paige, M., Papademetre, L. and Scarino, A. (2004) *Integrated Resources for Intercultural Teaching and Learning in the Context of Internationalisation in Higher Education*. Adelaide: Research Centre for Languages and Cultures Education, School of International Studies, University of South Australia. [http://www.unisanet.unisa.edu.au/learningconnection/staff/practice/internationalisation/documents/FINAL_REPORT.pdf]

Cullen, J. and St. George, A. (1996) 'Scripts for learning: Reflecting dynamics of classroom life'. *Journal for Australian Research in Early Childhood Education*, 1: 10–19.

de Haan, M.J. and Elbers, E.P.J.M. (2008) 'Diversity in the construction of modes of collaboration in multi-ethnic classrooms: Continuity and interruption of cultural scripts'. In B. Van Oers, W. Wardekker, E. Elbers and R. van der Veer (eds), *The Transformation of Learning: Perspectives from activity theory.* Cambridge: Cambridge University Press.

Fennes, H. and Hapgood, K. (1997) *Intercultural Learning in the Classroom: Crossing borders.* London: Cassell.

Fivush, R. (1984) 'Learning about school: the development of kindergartners' school script'. *Child Development*, 55: 1697–1709.

Geertz, C. (1975) *The Interpretation of Cultures.* London: Hutchinson.

Holstein, J.A. and Gubrium, J.F. (1995) *The Active Interview.* Thousand Oaks, CA: Sage.

Hvitfeldt, C. (1986) 'Traditional culture, perceptual style, and learning: The classroom behavior of Hmong adults'. *Adult Education Quarterly*, 36(2): 65–77.

Kember, D. (2000) 'Misconceptions about the learning approaches, motivation and study practices of Asian students'. *Higher Education*, 40(1): 99–121.

—(2001) 'Beliefs about knowledge and the process of teaching and learning as a factor in adjusting to study in higher education'. *Studies in Higher Education*, 26(2): 205–21.

Kettle, M. (2005) 'Agency as discursive practice: From "nobody" to "somebody" as an international student in Australia'. *Asia Pacific Journal of Education*, 25(1): 45–60.

Lord, R.G. and Kernan, M.C. (1987) 'Scripts as determinants of purposeful behavior in organizations'. *Academy of Management Review*, 12(2): 265–77.

Marton, F., Dall'Alba, G. and Beaty, E. (1993) 'Conceptions of learning'. *International Journal of Educational Research*, 19(3): 277–300.

Nelson, K. (ed.) (1986) *Event Knowledge: Structure and function in development.* Mahwah, NJ: Lawrence Erlbaum.

Samuelowicz, K. and Bain, J. (2001) 'Revisiting academics' beliefs about teaching and learning'. *Higher Education*, 41(3): 299–325.

Schank, R.C. and Abelson, R.P. (1977) *Scripts, Plans, Goals and Understanding: An inquiry into human knowledge structures.* Hillsdale, NJ: Erlbaum Associates.

Scollon, R. and Scollon, S.W. (1995) *Intercultural Communication: A discourse approach.* Oxford: Blackwell.

Stigler, J. and Hiebert, J. (1998) 'Teaching is a cultural activity'. *American Educator*, 22(4), 4–11.

Storti, C. (1990) *The Art of Crossing Cultures.* Yarmouth, ME: Intercultural Press.

Todd, E.S. (1997) 'Supervising overseas students'. In D. MacNamara and R. Harris (eds), *Overseas Students in Higher Education: Issues in teaching and learning.* London: Routledge.

Watkins, D. (2000) 'Learning and teaching: A cross-cultural perspective'. *School Leadership and Management*, 20(2): 161–73.

Welikala, T.C. (2006) 'Cultural scripts for learning in an intercultural higher education context: A narrative approach'. Unpublished PhD thesis, University of London.

Wierzbicka, A. (1998) 'German "cultural scripts": Public signs as a key to social attitudes and cultural values'. *Discourse and Society*, 9(2): 241–82.

Index